The Plot Thickens

by Chris Evans

*A collection of poems and thoughts dedicated to
the general public (and their mates).
The people who have inspired and encouraged me through life
often without knowing that they were doing it.
We've probably never even met,
but thank you.*

Published
by
REARDON PUBLISHING
56, Upper Norwood Street, Leckhampton,
Cheltenham, Glos, GL53 0DU
Website: www.reardon.co.uk

"For my Dad"

Written and Inspired
by
Chris Evans

ISBN 1 873877 49 8

Layout and Design
by
Nicholas Reardon

Cartoon Drawings
by
Chris Evans

Cover Design
by
Nicholas Reardon

Printed
by
Stoate & Bishop
Cheltenham

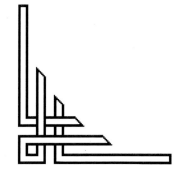
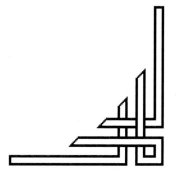

The Holiday Train.

Clackety Clack,Clackety Clack,
The holiday Train,
Runs down the track.
Holiday makers,
Escaping the rain,
Distracting the kids,
On the holiday Train.
A seaside attraction,
You can't ignore,
Steaming along,
Close to the shore.
All winds and weathers,
A job to be done,
Abducting the Tourist,
Searching for fun.
Packed in a carriage,
A fiver a time,
Savour the smoke,
As it shunts down the line.
Passing the Chip Shop,
Crossing the lane,
Children all wave,
From the holiday Train.
Sparkling Engine,
White picket fence,
Into the sand dunes,
Caravans and tents.
The whistle keeps blowing,
The dunes block the view,

Nothing to see,
Nothing to do.
Children have had it,
Dads feel the strain,
Babies are sick,
On the Holiday Train.
There in the Guide Book,
Top things to do,
A must for the kids,
There isn't a loo.
A Souvenir Pencil,
A book on the track,
That's the Holiday Train,
And thank God we're back.

The Holiday Train.

Things That Go Bump.

A crack in the Manifold,
Burned out clutch,
Riding on the pedal,
It wont cost much.
There goes the Silencer,
A hole in the sump,
Shock absorbers gone,
And there's another bump.

Suspension is collapsing,
Fuel consumptions high,
What's excess emission,
To a great big sky,
Steering rod is twisted,
The brakes are in doubt,
And here's another bump,
So I'd better watch out.

The engines over heating,
Now I can smell fuel,
To realign the tracking,
Needs a specialist tool,
I haven't been speeding,
I wont get the hump,
The exhausts dropped off,
And here's another bump.

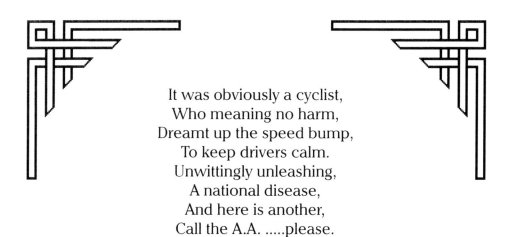

It was obviously a cyclist,
Who meaning no harm,
Dreamt up the speed bump,
To keep drivers calm.
Unwittingly unleashing,
A national disease,
And here is another,
Call the A.A. .....please.

Things That Go Bump.

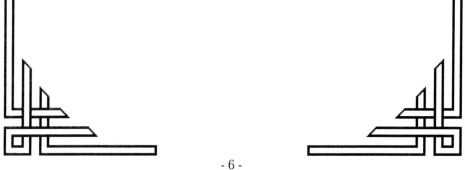

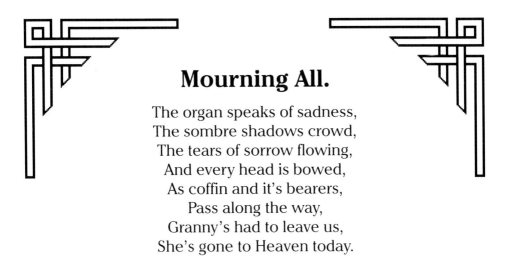

Mourning All.

The organ speaks of sadness,
The sombre shadows crowd,
The tears of sorrow flowing,
And every head is bowed,
As coffin and it's bearers,
Pass along the way,
Granny's had to leave us,
She's gone to Heaven today.

The Preacher offers comfort,
From his pulpit in the sky,
Granny's gone to be with God,
And to get there had to die.
The Vicar, with surplus breakfast,
Stained white against the black,
Coughs and calls for order,
Someone's laughing at the back.

"This Service is a celebration,
Of Granny's life on Earth,
She made the tea at cricket,
The home help knew her worth".
Then there was the Bingo,
And let us not forget,
Her love of Fags and Whiskey,
And how she liked to bet.

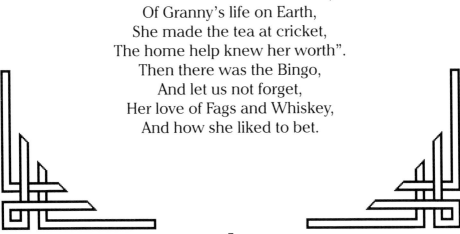

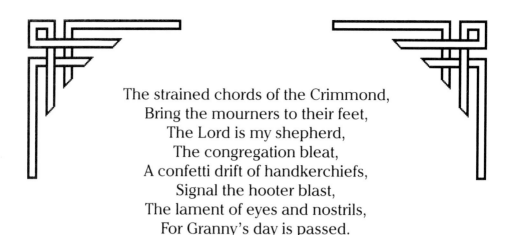

The strained chords of the Crimmond,
Bring the mourners to their feet,
The Lord is my shepherd,
The congregation bleat,
A confetti drift of handkerchiefs,
Signal the hooter blast,
The lament of eyes and nostrils,
For Granny's day is passed.

She's gone to be with Grandad,
I bet she's there by now,
Just hope he's not gone down the pub,
There'll be another row,
She was no saint herself of course,
And many things were said,
About a certain Milkman,
But no matter now, she's dead.

We all one day will take this path.
And all will leave their stains,
But somehow it doesn't matter,
When just a box remains,
A blessing on you Granny,
One last observation I'll record,
I see from the Order of Service,
That your real name was Maud............I'll stick to
Granny I think.

Mourning All.

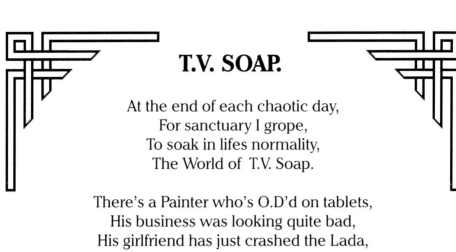

T.V. SOAP.

At the end of each chaotic day,
For sanctuary I grope,
To soak in lifes normality,
The World of T.V. Soap.

There's a Painter who's O.D'd on tablets,
His business was looking quite bad,
His girlfriend has just crashed the Lada,
Bought with cash she was left by her Dad,
Her mate is awaiting a sex change,
That is if she's let out of clink,
Her lover for days has been missing,
A possible murder they think,
His body has just been discovered,
In the yard at the back of the shop,
By a builder and part time stripper,
Though it's said that he isn't much cop.
His wife, a very bright lady,
With a double Mathematics degree,
Fosters kids that they rescued from Bosnia,
The eldest of whom's 43.
She's been having a fling with the Vicar,
A reformed alcoholic from Cheam,
Whose brother's a drug pushing Junkie,
And involved in a Tax dodging scheme,
That he hatched with the local Pub Landlord,
A fella that wont miss a trick,
Whose Mother is blind and Arthritic,
And wobbles along with a stick.
Her daughter, now there is a woman,
Bleached blonde and brazen no doubt,

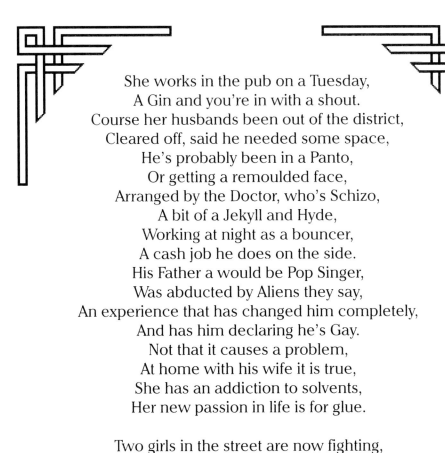

She works in the pub on a Tuesday,
A Gin and you're in with a shout.
Course her husbands been out of the district,
Cleared off, said he needed some space,
He's probably been in a Panto,
Or getting a remoulded face,
Arranged by the Doctor, who's Schizo,
A bit of a Jekyll and Hyde,
Working at night as a bouncer,
A cash job he does on the side.
His Father a would be Pop Singer,
Was abducted by Aliens they say,
An experience that has changed him completely,
And has him declaring he's Gay.
Not that it causes a problem,
At home with his wife it is true,
She has an addiction to solvents,
Her new passion in life is for glue.

Two girls in the street are now fighting,
The Painter's put under arrest,
His girlfriends mate with a tear in her eye,
Waits news of a D.N.A. test.
The Vicar is shopping for Vodka,
He's got Whiskey and Gin on his list,
There's a mugging, a rape and two break ins,
The next episode can't be missed.
And now a dog has been found in the Lada,
That crashed half an hour ago,
But you can't see the name on it's collar,
'til the start of tomorrow nights show.

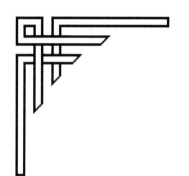

T.V. SOAP.

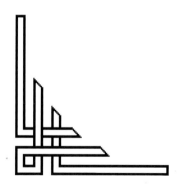

The Mystery.

I may not have seen it,
Although I'm not blind,
It's possible it happened,
A little way behind,
When I wasn't looking,
Or a lifetime before,
The whole host of things,
That I never saw.

I could have just missed it,
I was close it's true,
But what ever was,
Is now out of view,
But I find it exciting,
When I stand in a space,
Knowing things happened,
In this very place.

...................That's History.

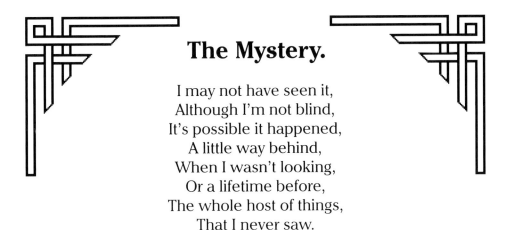

The Mystery.

On Monday.

On Monday I feel weary,
On Tuesday I'm worn out,
On Wednesday, drained of energy,
On Thursday good for nowt,
On Friday quite exhausted,
On Saturday things are bleak,
On Sunday, well, I'm shattered,
And that is me....all weak.

On Monday.

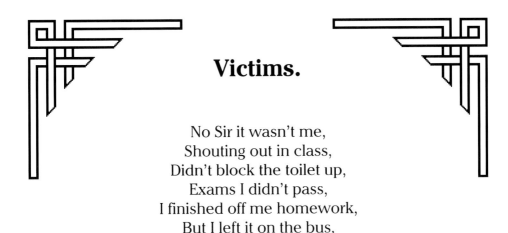

Victims.

No Sir it wasn't me,
Shouting out in class,
Didn't block the toilet up,
Exams I didn't pass,
I finished off me homework,
But I left it on the bus,
He started it, not me Sir,
But I wont make a fuss.

No Sir it wasn't me,
Tore pages out me book,
Haven't found me tie yet,
Me Mum helped me to look,
She couldn't telephone Sir,
She did give me a note,
But it got a little soggy,
When the rain got in me coat.

No Sir it wasn't me,
I never ever swear,
Me Dad would have me grounded,
I wouldn't ever dare,
What stud is that Sir?
I'll take it out me nose,
Sorry 'bout the Sweatshirt Sir,
I'm growin' out me clothes.

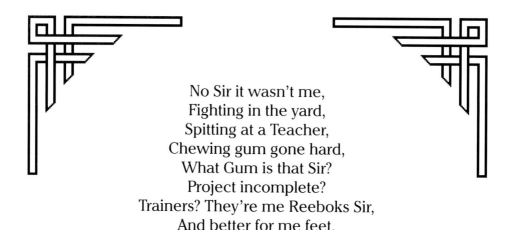

No Sir it wasn't me,
Fighting in the yard,
Spitting at a Teacher,
Chewing gum gone hard,
What Gum is that Sir?
Project incomplete?
Trainers? They're me Reeboks Sir,
And better for me feet.

No Sir it wasn't me,
Smoking by the gate,
Bike had a puncture,
That's why I'm three hours late,
Climbing on a table?
Graffiti on the wall?
I didn't see nothing Sir,
Not that I recall.

No Sir it wasn't me,
I didn't get detention,
Educations going well,
Without your intervention,
You seem a bit frustrated Sir,
See I'm a lot like you,
A victim of the system,
So now what shall we do?

No Sir it wasn't me,
No Sir it wasn't me,
No Sir it wasn't me..............I think it was you.

Victims.

For Teachers Everywhere

I Went To Town.

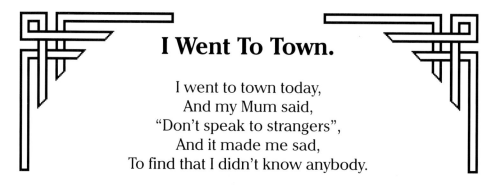

I went to town today,
And my Mum said,
"Don't speak to strangers",
And it made me sad,
To find that I didn't know anybody.

I went to town today,
And my Mum said,
"Don't speak to strange people"
And because nobody spoke to me,
It made me wonder if I was strange.

I went to town today,
It was full of people,
Worrying about strangers and,
Wondering if it was them,
That was strange.

Today I spoke to everybody.

I Went To Town.

A Good Knight
Out.

So, where is my knighthood?
That's what I want to know,
After all I've done for Britain,
Surely it's my go.

Ok, so I'm not English,
But my mother was a Scot,
My father was from the Continent,
But a Nazi he was not.

I've made my home in England,
Well, only one it's true,
For arts sake I'm in Hollywood,
Where the Tax man can't get you.

My heart though is with the British,
My devoted, adoring fans.
They think I should be knighted,
So it must be on the plans.

The Royals are all friends of mine,
They know me from the screen,
And my appearance on the Honours list,
Will not surprise the Queen.

True, I'm not a Royalist,
But I'm a Patron of A wildlife trust,
I attend premieres for Charity,
am seen with the upper crust.

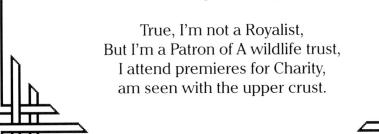

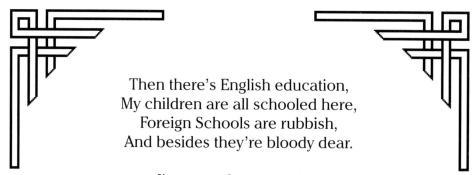

Then there's English education,
My children are all schooled here,
Foreign Schools are rubbish,
And besides they're bloody dear.

I'm a regular supporter,
Of the good old National Health,
I hold a British Passport,
So needn't squander hard earned wealth.

I know there has been gossip,
Stars always make good news,
That substance was not identified,
And I'm almost off the booze.

Ok, so I've had Mistresses,
And the odd paternity suit,
But my third wife understands me,
I'm a Millionaire to boot.

So come on you Politicians,
It's a Knighthood I deserve,
I could bolster up the party fund,
Don't hold me in reserve.

Just stick me on the Honours list,
You know it's only right,
I've an MBE already,
Now I want to be a Knight.

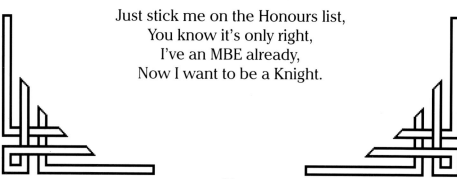

*A Good Knight
Out.*

In Praise of 'Entitlement'

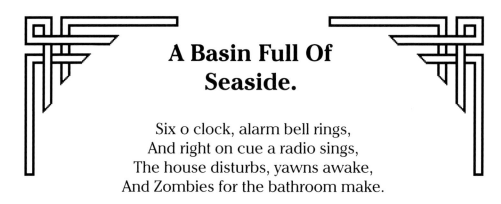

A Basin Full Of Seaside.

Six o clock, alarm bell rings,
And right on cue a radio sings,
The house disturbs, yawns awake,
And Zombies for the bathroom make.

Fighting over toilet space,
Scrubbing teeth and licking face,
"Come on you kids, get in the car",
And outside voices shout "we are".

Locking windows, check the door,
"Dad, I need the loo" once more,
"Move up Michael, alright, it's a squeeze",
And "Will you get that belt on please?"

Off to the Garage, check the air,
Mother smiles and thinks it rare,
Whilst children shuffle in their seats,
And hope that Dad is buying Sweets.

The Navigator checks the map,
That's upside down across her lap,
The key is turned, a teasing cough,
Mirror adjusted and they're off.

The long awaited trips begun,
The Seaside outing full of fun.

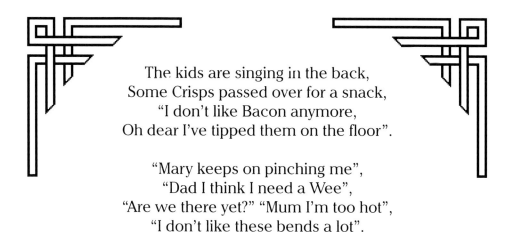

The kids are singing in the back,
Some Crisps passed over for a snack,
"I don't like Bacon anymore,
Oh dear I've tipped them on the floor".

"Mary keeps on pinching me",
"Dad I think I need a Wee",
"Are we there yet?" "Mum I'm too hot",
"I don't like these bends a lot".

"I spy with my little eye,
Something runny that starts with Y,
Yuck...urgh Dad pull in quick",
Too late Tommy's just been sick.

"You should have turned off right back there",
"Mummy I heard Daddy swear".

At last, at last we spy the sea,
And everybody shrieks with glee,
The car gets parked a mile away,
Five pound on the Prom too much to pay.

So the procession winds its way,
With all that's needed for the day,
The Beach Ball, Wind Break, Lilo, Chair,
The Picnic and warm clothes to wear.

You really never can be sure,
About weather forecasts anymore.

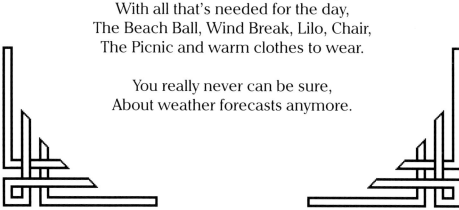

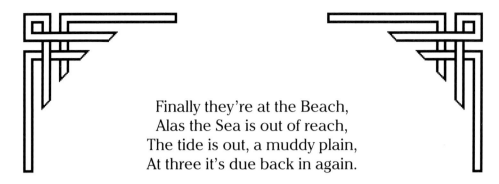

Finally they're at the Beach,
Alas the Sea is out of reach,
The tide is out, a muddy plain,
At three it's due back in again.

And so they camp, this happy lot,
Dumping gear to mark their spot,
Between the reddening rows of flesh,
In various states of cautiousness.

They settle.

"Grandad cover up your head,
The bald bits going very red",
"Careful burying your brother dear,
Just try to keep his nostrils clear".

"Can we have an Ice Cream yet?"
"Did we bring the Cricket set?"
"Well, really Roger, look down there",
Todays young people just don't care.

"Have you seen the size of that?"
"Him with the Hanky for a hat?"
"And he's hardly made for that String Vest,
Blocks the view for all the rest".

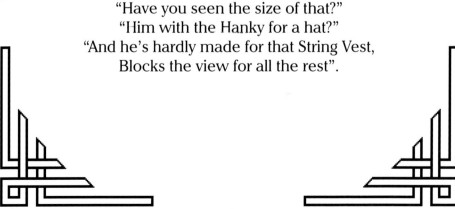

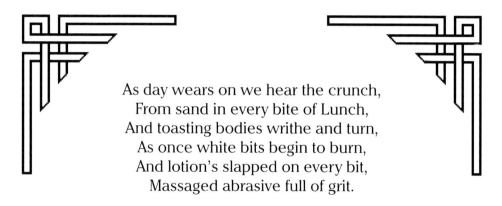

As day wears on we hear the crunch,
From sand in every bite of Lunch,
And toasting bodies writhe and turn,
As once white bits begin to burn,
And lotion's slapped on every bit,
Massaged abrasive full of grit.

Whilst Fathers with Binoculars,
Check half clad girls particulars,
An angry Wasp stings lollied lip,
As sea chilled children stand and drip.....on
Grandad.

"Can we have an Ice Cream Dad?"
The day is nearly through,
The lady in the Anorak,
Now so cold she's blue.

The shaken towelling sand storm sweeps across the
shore,
The Ice Cream van is ringing and the children ask
once more.

Sitting on the Quayside, Ice Cream in the hand,
Melting over fingers, dripping memories on the
sand.

Then flocking from the Sea front, a thousand driven
sheep,
Homeward bound 'til next year,
For now, it's time to sleep.

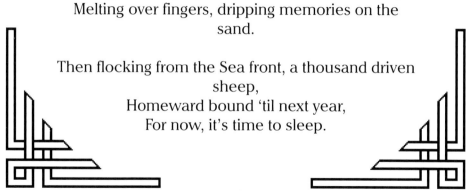

A Basin Full Of Seaside.

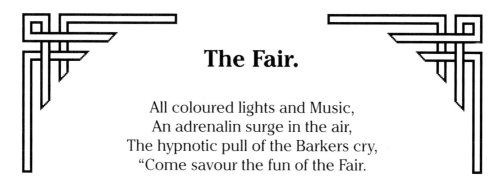

The Fair.

All coloured lights and Music,
An adrenalin surge in the air,
The hypnotic pull of the Barkers cry,
"Come savour the fun of the Fair.

There's a crowd and the kids tug me forward,
"Roll up, just 50p a go,
Everyone's a winner love,
Come on now give it a throw".

Knee deep the mud and the sawdust,
The screams from a ride overhead,
The guaranteed Taiwanese prizes,
Or a fish for three darts in a bed.

There's a ping, ping, ping as the pellets,
From distorted guns miss their mark,
The Coconut shy, with a man with one eye,
It's a nightmare in our local Park.

Stands of Burgers and translucent Onions,
Congealed condiment caps hint at sauce,
A shower of sparks, the Bumper Cars dance,
To the joy of the Merry go Horse.

As onward ever onward,
'Til all trace of normality's gone,
And I stand in front of the Waltzers,
The kids shrieking are pulling me on.

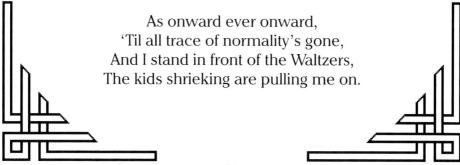

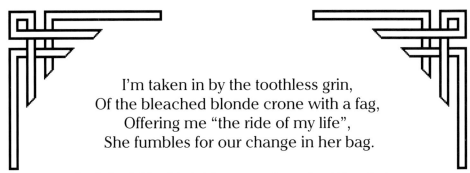

I'm taken in by the toothless grin,
Of the bleached blonde crone with a fag,
Offering me "the ride of my life",
She fumbles for our change in her bag.

And the kids think it's great, they don't hesitate,
And in the wink of a blood shot eye,
We're strapped in a chair, by a muscle with no hair.
No chance for a last goodbye.

Then the music cranks, the ride is off,
A gentle rolling sea,
Up and down and round and round,
Not as bad as I thought it would be.

'Til the muscle bound jerk sets about his work,
Gives an almighty spin,
And the harmless ride has me terrified,
But I'm tough and I can't give in.

Faster and faster and up and down,
A Carnival Waterloo,
Elvis sings out and the kids all shout,
Will they stop if I ask them to?

I'm loosing my grip, my hands start to slip,
What the hell am I doing on here?
My balance is shot, I can't see a lot,
And my stomach is feeling quite queer.

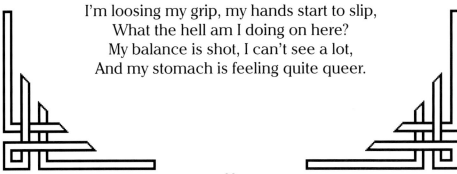

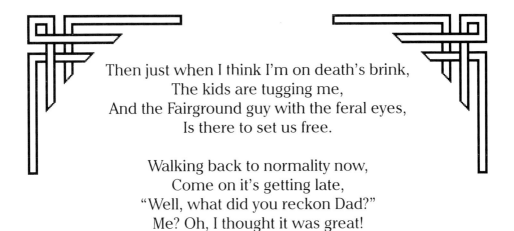

Then just when I think I'm on death's brink,
The kids are tugging me,
And the Fairground guy with the feral eyes,
Is there to set us free.

Walking back to normality now,
Come on it's getting late,
"Well, what did you reckon Dad?"
Me? Oh, I thought it was great!

I do hate lying to those kids.

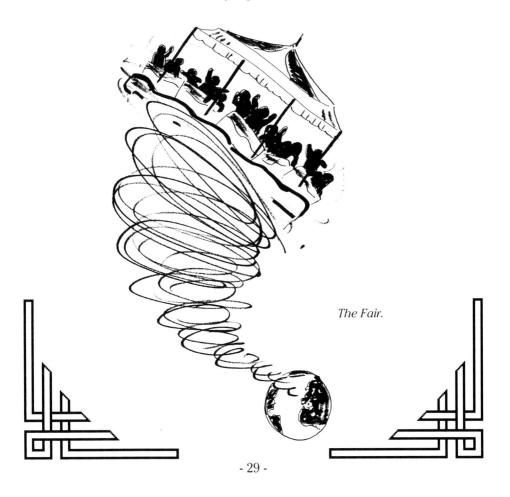

The Fair.

Heavens Hell Drivers.

Coughing through a cloud of dust,
Car impatient, tearing by,
Around the corner who knows what,
A short cut to the sky?

No, Heavens hand is guiding here,
A Mission that can't wait,
Two Nuns in a Ford Capri,
Flying 'cos they're late.

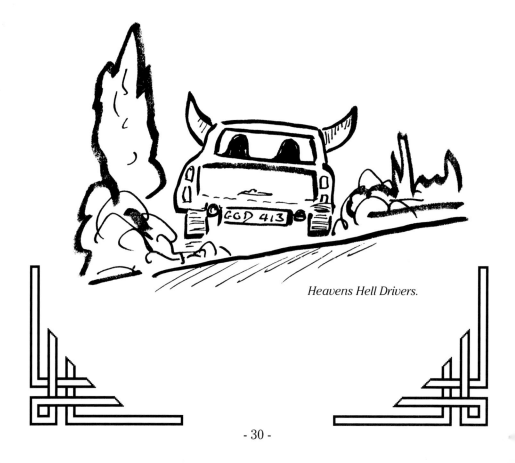

Heavens Hell Drivers.

Patients Please.

A routine trip to the Doctors,
" I'm sorry Sir, you'll have to wait"
The waiting room full of sick Sardines,
The Doctor is running quite late.
Row upon row of illness,
And me jammed up tight with the rest,
A blending of hacking and snuffles,
Of phlegm being drawn from the chest.
A man with a boil on his elbow,
Another with a clear case of Gout,
Whilst the woman whose bosom I'm nudging,
Has a problem that she's just let out.
Two children with matted up nostrils,
Are throwing magazines on the floor,
An OAP in the corner, dozing off,
Has now started to snore.
The heating is up to a hundred,
A TCP smell fills the air,
The man with the terminal cancer,
Stares up to the sky in despair.
Ignoring the girl with the Measles,
And the chap with pituatry eyes,
Who appears to stare at another,
Whose blood pressure's starting to rise.
And here I am stuck in the middle,
With a lady armed with a stick,
Unwittingly offering protection,
From the Tramp who has now just been sick.
To add to the general commotion,
A mobile is starting to ring,
From somewhere inside of the jacket,

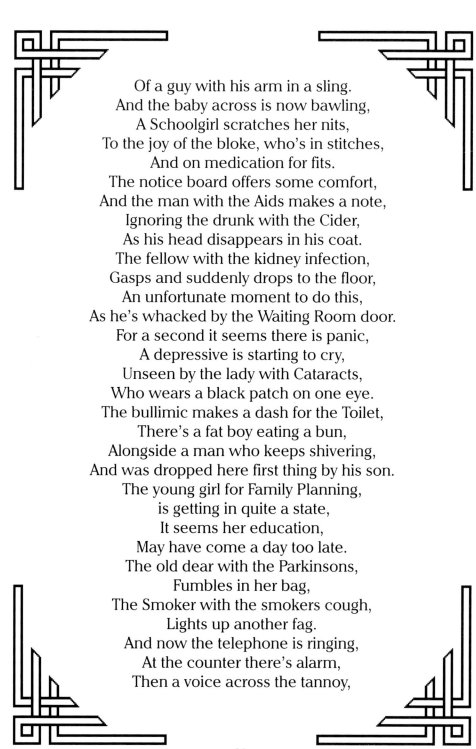

Of a guy with his arm in a sling.
And the baby across is now bawling,
A Schoolgirl scratches her nits,
To the joy of the bloke, who's in stitches,
And on medication for fits.
The notice board offers some comfort,
And the man with the Aids makes a note,
Ignoring the drunk with the Cider,
As his head disappears in his coat.
The fellow with the kidney infection,
Gasps and suddenly drops to the floor,
An unfortunate moment to do this,
As he's whacked by the Waiting Room door.
For a second it seems there is panic,
A depressive is starting to cry,
Unseen by the lady with Cataracts,
Who wears a black patch on one eye.
The bullimic makes a dash for the Toilet,
There's a fat boy eating a bun,
Alongside a man who keeps shivering,
And was dropped here first thing by his son.
The young girl for Family Planning,
is getting in quite a state,
It seems her education,
May have come a day too late.
The old dear with the Parkinsons,
Fumbles in her bag,
The Smoker with the smokers cough,
Lights up another fag.
And now the telephone is ringing,
At the counter there's alarm,
Then a voice across the tannoy,

Theatrically calm.
"Here is a special announcement,
I am sorry to have to say,
That the Doctor has a Migraine,
So he won't be in today".

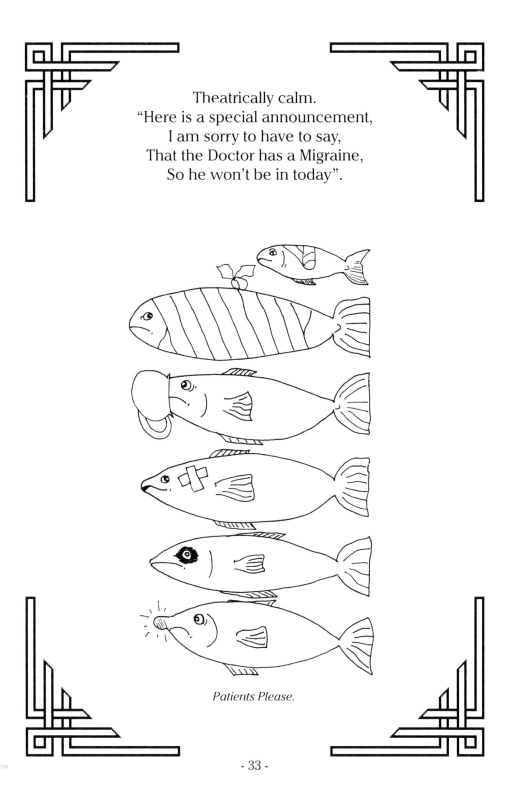

Patients Please.

No Reply Came The Answer.

"Sorry we are unable to take your call right now, but
if you leave your name and number,
we'll get back to you".

Oh, not an Answerphone,
They put me in a flap,
My thoughts go into hiding,
Locked in some mental trap.

My vocabulary has been shuffled,
My communication chords have snapped,
I'm never ever stuck for words,
But my dictionary's been scrapped.

The thought process quite scrambled,
What's happened to the Brain,
The linking of one sentence,
Causes cerebral pain.

How totally ridiculous,
I just can't find a word,
The mouth can make the movement,
But not a sound is heard.

It's no use, I can't do it,
This really is insane,
So, I'll hang up, rehearse myself,
And then I'll try again.

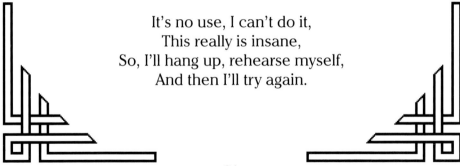

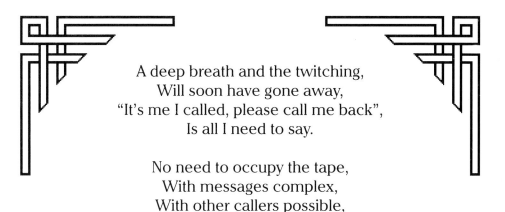

A deep breath and the twitching,
Will soon have gone away,
"It's me I called, please call me back",
Is all I need to say.

No need to occupy the tape,
With messages complex,
With other callers possible,
A monologue will vex.

So, I'll keep it really simple,
That's the best way I am sure,
Just my name and number,
And really nothing more.

Well, here we go, I'm practised,
I won't waiver from my track,
"Hello, hello who is this ?"
Oh bugger it they're back.

*No Reply
Came The Answer.*

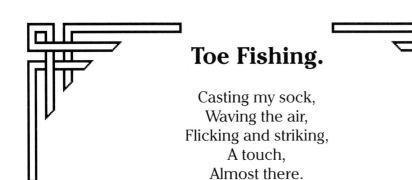

Toe Fishing.

Casting my sock,
Waving the air,
Flicking and striking,
A touch,
Almost there.

Twisting and casting,
Then twisting again,
The tear on my cheek,
Confirming the pain.

Casting my sock,
Frustrated it's true,
Altered position,
I'll try something new.

Curling and Bending,
By chance I've a catch,
A cry of despair,
As toes shrug my snatch.

Casting my sock,
My toes now so near,
I'll get this sock on,
Independence is dear.

Distortion,
Contortion,
A spasm, a yelp,
Been trying for ages,
"Stop laughing and help !"

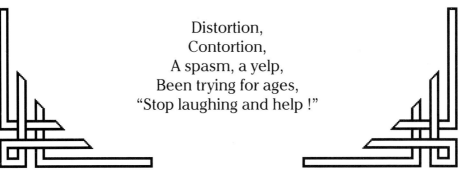

Toe Fishing.

Dedicated to Back Sufferers Everywhere

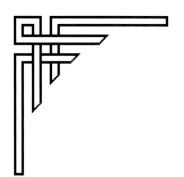
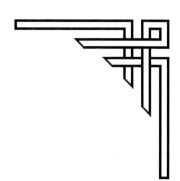

A Man Has Died.

A man has died,
A child is born today,
The Sun comes up,
To break the cloud,

And the dust,................... just blows away.

Once you get used to it, it's gone.

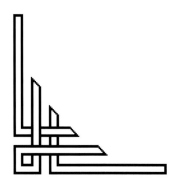

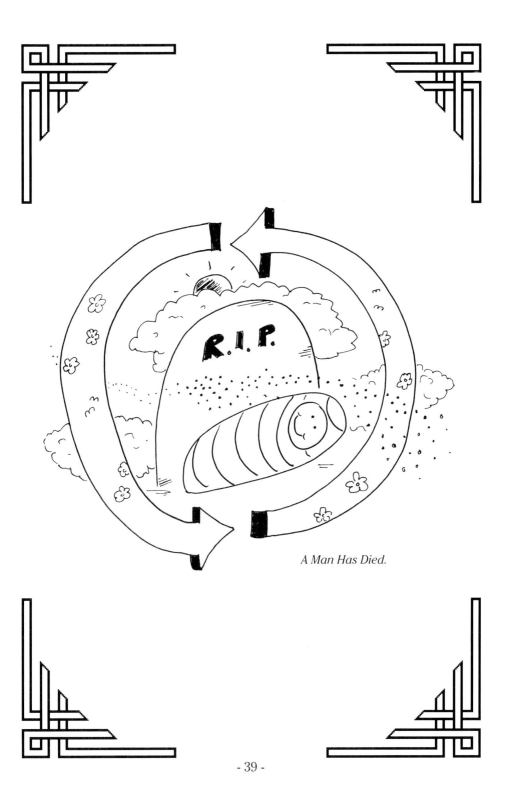

A Man Has Died.

ISBN 1-873877-07-2

THE
VEGETABLE
LOVERS

GUIDE

If you have enjoyed this book then why not try
an unusual poetic celebration of the
characters we call vegetables
also by
Chris Evans